The Cuban Americans

LAURA M. HAHN

MAJOR AMERICAN IMMIGRATION

MASON CREST PUBLISHERS • PHILADELPHIA

The island of Cuba boasts lush and fertile farmland. Many people make their living from agriculture in this poor Caribbean nation.

The Cuban Americans

LAURA M. HAHN

MAJOR AMERICAN IMMIGRATION

MASON CREST PUBLISHERS • PHILADELPHIA

Mason Crest Publishers
370 Reed Road
Broomall PA 19008
www.masoncrest.com

Copyright © 2009 by Mason Crest Publishers. All rights reserved.
Printed and bound in Malaysia.

First printing

1 3 5 7 9 8 6 4 2

Library of Congress Cataloging-in-Publication Data

Hahn, Laura.
  The Cuban Americans / Laura M. Hahn.
      p. cm. — (Major American immigration)
  Includes bibliographical references and index.
  ISBN-13: 978-1-4222-0606-5 (hardcover)
  ISBN-10: 1-4222-0606-8 (hardcover)
  ISBN-13: 978-1-4222-0673-7 (pbk.)
  ISBN-10: 1-4222-0673-4 (pbk.)
  1. Cuban Americans—History—Juvenile literature. 2. Cuban
Americans—Juvenile literature. 3. Immigrants—United States—
Juvenile literature. I. Title.
  E184.C97H342 2008
  973'.004687291—dc22
                                        2008026014

Table of Contents

MAJOR AMERICAN IMMIGRATION

America's Ethnic Heritage

Barry Moreno, librarian
Statue of Liberty/
Ellis Island National Monument

E thnic diversity is one of the most striking characteristics of the American identity. In the United States the Bureau of the Census officially recognizes 122 different ethnic groups. North America's population had grown by leaps and bounds, starting with the American Indian tribes and nations—the continent's original people— and increasing with the arrival of the European colonial migrants who came to these shores during the 16th and 17th centuries. Since then, millions of immigrants have come to America from every corner of the world.

But the passage of generations and the great distance of America from the "Old World"—Europe, Africa, and Asia—has in some cases separated immigrant peoples from their roots. The struggle to succeed in America made it easy to forget past traditions. Further, the American spirit of freedom, individualism, and equality gave Americans a perspective quite different from the view of life shared by residents of the Old World.

Immigrants of the 19th and 20th centuries recognized this at once. Many tried to "Americanize" themselves by tossing away their peasant clothes and dressing American-style even before reaching their new homes in the cities or the countryside of America. It was not so easy to become part of America's culture, however. For many immigrants, learning English was quite a hurdle. In fact, most older immigrants clung to the old ways, preferring to speak their native languages and follow their familiar customs and traditions. This was easy to do when ethnic neighborhoods abounded in large North American cities like New York, Montreal, Philadelphia, Chicago, Toronto, Boston, Cleveland, St. Louis, New Orleans and San Francisco. In rural areas, farm families—many of them Scandinavian, German, or Czech—established their own tightly knit communities. Thus foreign languages and dialects, religious beliefs, Old World customs, and certain class distinctions flourished.

The most striking changes occurred among the children of immigrants, whose hopes and dreams were different from those of their parents. They began breaking away from the Old World customs, perhaps as a reaction to the embarrassment of being labeled "foreigner." They badly wanted to be Americans, and assimilated more easily than their parents and grandparents. They learned to speak English without a foreign accent, to dress and act like other Americans. The assimilation of the children of immigrants was encouraged by social contact—games, schools, jobs, and military service—which further broke down the barriers between immigrant groups and hastened the process of Americanization. Along the way, many family traditions were lost or abandoned.

Today, the pride that Americans have in their ethnic roots is one of the abiding strengths of both the United States and Canada. It shows that the theory which called America a "melting pot" of the world's people was never really true. The thought that a single "American" would emerge from the combination of these peoples has never happened, for Americans have grown more reluctant than ever before to forget the struggles of their ethnic forefathers. The growth of cultural studies and genealogical research indicates that Americans are anxious not to entirely lose this identity, whether it is English, French, Chinese, African, Mexican, or some other group. There is an interest in tracing back the family line as far as records or memory will take them. In a sense, this has made Americans a divided people; proud to be Americans, but proud also of their ethnic roots.

As a result, many Americans have welcomed a new identity, that of the hyphenated American. This unique description has grown in usage over the years and continues to grow as more Americans recognize the importance of family heritage. In the end, this is an appreciation of America's great cultural heritage and its richness of its variety.

About 43 percent of Cuba's cultivatable land is reserved for sugar plantations. Cuban farmers produce 5 million tons of sugar each year.

A Family's Flight from Cuba

In 1980, a young girl of 14 arrived in the United States on a large boat packed with people from her homeland of Cuba. Marisol was alone and scared and unsure of what would happen next. Surrounded by strange faces, she huddled in a corner on the boat's deck as it crossed the 90 miles of water between the island of Cuba to Key West, Florida, one of the islands in the string at the southern end of the United States. Listening to the excited voices around her, she kept her eyes shut to quiet her stomach's churning and hold back her tears. As the boat moved across the sea, pulling her further away from her homeland, her mother, and all that she knew, Marisol recalled her life prior to this and everything that brought her to this moment on the boat.

Before that day, she had lived in a small apartment in Havana— going to school and helping her mother sew clothes when she got home. Marisol's mother sewed at the factory during the day, but at night, to make extra money, she made beautiful clothes for special clients—such as the wives of government officials. While the factory job paid her mother very little, the special clients paid her quite a lot for the gowns and dresses she created. It was because of this money that occasionally Marisol got some fresh fruit or an extra pair of shoes. But whenever Marisol received a treat, her mother told her to keep it secret. "There are spies all around," her mother often whispered as they walked to the store with their heads tucked down. "You must never talk about your good fortune, Marisol. Just keep quiet, and look like everybody else."

During those evening hours, behind closed shades and locked doors, as Marisol sewed beads onto beautiful cloth, her mother would sing sad songs and tell Marisol stories of growing up on a sugarcane plantation in a big house with her parents. She told her how Marisol's mother and father and brother left the plantation, moving to Havana after Fidel Castro took over Cuba. Stories of how Marisol's father and brother were put into jail for trying to escape Cuba when Marisol was only four. Marisol often dreamed at night about dancing with her father and her grandfather in the big house surrounded by sugarcane fields as her mother sang happy songs in a strong, loud voice.

Then, on an April day in 1980, everything changed. While sitting in her schoolroom, Marisol was surprised when her mother arrived and took her out of school. They ran down Havana's streets until they arrived at the Peruvian Embassy. To Marisol's eyes, it was like a big fiesta. Ten thousand people were jammed into the compound. The Cuban guards who normally guarded the gates were gone, and the crowd was yelling for Castro to let them leave Cuba to earn money for themselves and have a better life. Most of the people at the Embassy had recently been visited by relatives who were allowed to return to Cuba for the first time since emigrating in 1960. One hundred thousand relatives came in 1979, bringing with them televisions and socks and stockings and dresses and foods that no one on the island of Cuba had seen for decades. The riches from the outside world that those visitors brought changed the way the people on the island of Cuba thought about their lives. They saw the freedom their relatives enjoyed. The Cubans who were not allowed to leave the island since Castro took over the government now wanted that same freedom for themselves.

In the midst of all this commotion, Marisol clung to her mother's arm as they squeezed into the crowd. Marisol was dizzy from the heat by the time Fidel Castro came to the embassy to assure the people they would be granted *visas* to leave the country. The next few months were a blur to Marisol. Then, in late August, Marisol awoke in the morning to find her mother packing a suitcase. She filled it with the few clothes Marisol owned and a tattered book of photographs—the only ones left from her mother's childhood. "Hurry, Marisol," she said, "Great-Aunt Benita is coming soon, and you will take a journey to America for a better life."

A Cuban boy fills a bag with cotton on a plantation. Today, about 20 percent of Cubans work in agriculture.

Family is one of the most important
aspects of Cuban culture. It is not
uncommon for extended family to live
together under one roof.

Marisol did not see her mother's bag and asked why. "I cannot go," she answered. "Your father and brother would have no one to get them out of jail. I must stay until they are free. But you go to your Great-Aunt Nina's and begin a better life. We will catch up soon."

Then, Great-Aunt Benita came and took Marisol to Port Mariel. The docks were crazy with activity. People were everywhere, crowding the gangplanks to get on one of the many boats. Then, in a crush of people, Marisol was suddenly on a boat, alone. Looking down at the dock, Marisol did not understand why Great-Aunt Benita was still on land, crying and waving as the boat pulled away.

When the boat landed in Key West, Florida, there were thousands more people already there. Unlike her mother, Marisol had never learned to speak English. In fact, after the Castro Revolution, her mother had never spoken English in public again. To do so was to put them in danger of being suspected as antigovernment rebels by the Castro spies that lived in every neighborhood. So Marisol could not understand the directions from the "Americanos" who met them at the boat. She recalled her great aunt telling her to "pay attention" and "be good" and slipping a small piece of paper into her pocket just before she pushed Marisol onto the boat. Marisol watched what others were doing. She gathered her suitcase and followed the crowd into a "camp" surrounded by a chain-linked fence to wait for her rescue. As she wandered around the camp listening to snatches of conversation, she heard people talking about their relatives in the United States and showing pieces of paper to the Americanos.

Marisol pulled out the paper her aunt had slipped into her pocket and read it for the first time. It contained two names:

Nina Sanchez—Grandmother—New Jersey
Gustavo Perez—Cousin—Florida

Marisol stood in line for many hours until it was her turn. She then handed her paper to the lady at the table, who asked her some questions she did not understand. The woman standing in line behind Marisol began to translate: "They want to know where in New Jersey your grandmother lives." Marisol could only shrug. She didn't know how she could have a grandmother in New Jersey when the only grandmother she ever knew had died when she was six. Marisol had also never heard of any place called New Jersey. ✹

Many Cubans still live in modest homes in the countryside. The roof of this home was thatched with dried palm leaves.

The sale of Cuban cigars is a thriving business worldwide. Factory workers in Cuba earn less per day than the price of one cigar in Europe.

Marisol's Family in Cuba

By 1980, the family Marisol was born into had lived in Cuba for over 100 years. Her great, great, great, great-grandfather Juan Sanchez **immigrated** to Cuba from Spain in 1830. He was 10 years old and born into a fine Spanish family, but became **discontent** with the social life in Spain. He did not like parties and dances. He preferred adventure and the outdoors, so he convinced his father to let him seek his fortune in the sugar plantations. All his life, Juan had heard about the beautiful tropical island that Christopher Columbus discovered in 1492 and claimed for Spain. The word of this paradise spread, and soon Spaniards began to immigrate to build a new life on the island of Cuba. Over the **centuries**, the Cuban native Indians died off and Cuba became populated by people from other places. Between 1500 and 1800, the island's population grew from 6,000 to 250,000.

A Spaniard who moved to Cuba was called a *peninsular* and became part of the Spanish ruling class. Juan Sanchez did not care about the title or the society. He was a hard-working young man who kept busy buying land in Cuba and building a large plantation. When he died, Juan passed the plantation on to his son and grandsons, who passed it onto their children, including Marisol's great-grandfather, Martino Miguel Sanchez, born in 1890.

By 1908, when Marisol's great-grandfather Martino was 18 years old, the family plantation grew not only sugarcane but also tobacco for Cuban cigars. Since 1860, Cuban cigar factories had been established in Florida and New York City. Since the factory owners were Cuban, they wanted Cuban workers to hand-roll the cigars and do other factory jobs. This provided the poorer Cubans with an opportunity to improve their lives. By 1900, 11,000 working-class Cubans immigrated to the United States to work in the cigar factories.

During Marisol's great-grandfather's young adult years, there were many changes occurring in Cuban politics, ownership, and economics. The U.S. invested heavily in land and cattle. Spaniards kept immigrating and buying more land rights. In 1914, Americans discovered Cuba as a heavenly vacation spot with casinos, nightclubs, and sparkling beaches. The tourist industry brought a good income to the Cuban middle class, who provided many services for the tourists.

These growing economic conditions kept the upper and middle classes happy, so they had no desire to leave Cuba. But the poorest level of Cuban society—the greatest *majority* by far—was discontent; they had no voice and no money to either change Cuba or leave it.

Marisol's grandfather, Miguel, his brother Juan, and sister Benita enjoyed a life of wealth. Their cupboards were full of fine food and clothing. They went to parties and dances and traveled to Europe, South America, and the United States. The Sanchez children, like all of the Cuban *elite*, attended private schools, learned English, and continued the family's long history of a protected, happy life on the plantation.

Fulgencio Batista, former president of Cuba, relaxes outside his home. Batista ruled the island nation twice, from 1933 to 1944 and from 1952 to 1959, when he was overthrown by the revolutionary leader Fidel Castro.

Born on a sugar plantation in 1926, Fidel Castro became one of the last outspoken supporters of Communism. Due to his political affiliation, the United States has cut off trade with Cuba.

Great-Uncle Juan married Nina and moved to New York City to take over a cigar-making plant. Great-Aunt Benita married, bore a son, and moved to the Cuban city of Havana with her husband to begin a food distribution warehouse business. Marisol's grandfather, Miguel, was the only one to stay on the plantation. His wife gave birth to Marisol's mother, Marita, in 1941.

For Cuba, the 1940s were a time of high tourism and government policies that helped the rich get richer and the poor get poorer. Marisol's mother grew up on a protected and well-provided plantation, so she was *oblivious* to the rising discontent that the majority of Cubans felt about the limitations and poverty in their lives and the constant *turmoil* in the Cuban government. Between 1909 and 1959, Cuba was ruled by many politicians, one right after another. During Marita's youth, one leader became the strongest. Fulgencio Batista controlled the army and the country for nearly 18 years. Under Batista's control, unemployment rose to 20 percent while wages fell

WORDS FROM A CUBAN REVOLUTIONARY

"I was very much aware that the country needed social reforms in many areas. And as I read materials that Fidel Castro had written, I became more aware that this was an answer for the things that I had seen in the countryside. I saw it also as an answer for the poor people in the city who were experiencing a lot of hardships in terms of everyday living. . . . All our problems were going to be over then. Finally, the revolution had succeeded, and things were going to change, and we were going to be equal—equality for all people on the island—and everything was going to be peaceful and quiet from now on."

ISLAND OF CUBA

Discovered by Columbus in 1492, Cuba was claimed for Spain by Diego Velazquez in 1511. Spain would rule Cuba for the next 400 years, imposing its language, culture, and the Roman Catholic religion on Cuba until granting it independence in 1898. The United States then influenced Cuba for the next 50 years until Castro's reign. The 800-mile-long island is 160 miles wide in the east and 25 miles wide in the west. The coastal lowlands consist of swamps, peat bogs, heavy jungles, and mangrove trees. The central interior is less fertile, but there are large-scale agricultural regions in the western regions. The tropical climate has a rainy season from May to October.

20 percent and prices for food and clothing rose. Cuba soon had a *cost of living* that was the highest in the world. With no social services to help the poor, the streets became full of homeless, beggars, *peddlers*, thieves, and pickpockets. Crime shot up. Sugar production declined, and there were shortages of oil, gasoline, and transportation. All of this contributed to scaring off the tourists, who had brought a lot of money to Cuba. In 1952, Batista set up a *police state*, outlawing free speech and any criticism of political leaders. While this silenced many people, there were rebels who would not be quiet and spoke up against a government that only helped the rich. One of those rebels was Fidel Castro.

Castro was a bright young man from a poor background. His poverty, however, did not get in the way of his determination. Unlike many of his peers, he not only graduated high school but also college. Instead of going to work for a company, he organized other poor rebels against the Batista army. Soon, he was thrown into jail for two years for his actions. When he was released in 1955, he went right back to work, building momentum for a revolution against the oppressive government. He preached against being treated like third-class citizens, and the poor people of Cuba welcomed his message. Of the six million people who lived in Cuba, five million were in the working class—and they believed Fidel Castro could give them a better future. Secretly, the poor plantation workers organized a revolution across the island.

In 1959, Fidel Castro and his rebels marched out of the mountains, defeated Batista, and took over the Cuban government. Castro immediately changed Cuba's economy by slashing rents and utility rates, passing a minimum-wage law, and limiting land holdings. This action shocked the rich and brought cheers from the poor. The United States, however, did not like Castro's actions and cut off *economic relations* with the country.

In response, Cuba made an alliance with the Soviet Union, an enemy of the U.S. at the time. Cuba then adopted *communistic* principles. This included such things as no private ownership of land or businesses. Everyone was supposed to share equally both in the production and distribution of wealth.

That change threatened the existence of the upper class. For the first time in Cuba's history, people fled the island in *mass exile*. Unlike the typical immigrant from most countries, however, the people who were exiled from Cuba between 1959 and 1965 were not the poorest seeking a better life, but the wealthiest. They were called the Golden Exiles because of their wealth, their homes, their businesses, and their bank accounts—most of which they had to leave behind.

During that time, 250,000 people fled Cuba, taking with them only what they could carry. They fled to the United States—Miami, New York, and New Orleans in particular—and called upon the United States government to help them.

For the Sanchez family, it was a frightening change. By 1965, the plantation had been taken away by the government. Grandfather Martino continued to work the plantation, but no longer owned any of the profits or the land. All the money went to the government. Great-Aunt Benita and Jose's food warehouse was also taken over by the government. Their son Roberto fled to Miami, Florida with his wife and son. Great-Uncle Juan and Great-Aunt Nina lost their direct connection to Cuban tobacco and had to shut down their successful cigar manufacturing plant in New York City and move across the river to a less expensive area in New Jersey to find other work. Marita and Ramos moved from the plantation to Havana with their son to find work. Ramos took a job on the docks working with the fishing vessels. Marita worked in a sewing factory. Marita did not intend to get pregnant with Marisol in 1966, for she did not trust the new Cuba. Everything they had known had been taken away, and in its place were fear and food shortages and spies in every neighborhood, reporting anything that might be considered antigovernment. In 1970, desperate

The city of Havana is Cuba's most important port. Although the United States does not allow its citizens to visit Cuba, many visitors come by way of an indirect route such as Canada or Mexico.

to find a better way of living, Ramos took a chance to escape on a boat with his 11-year-old son. Marita would not go because Marisol was too young. Ramos and his son were caught, however, and jailed, leaving only Marita to care for Marisol.

Unlike her mother's youth of private schools and beautiful dresses and dances and travel, Marisol attended public school, often taught by people who were not trained teachers. She knew no other lifestyle, except from the stories her mother told her. She also heard about life in the United States from her Great-Aunt Benita and her grandmother. They all said it was a wonderful place to visit with many beautiful things to buy. But they always added that before the Castro revolution, Cuba was the most beautiful place of all to live with its sparkling beaches and forests and tropical flowers and music. Marisol had never heard the music or seen the beautiful beaches her relatives spoke about because Havana was no longer a city rich with booming businesses and wealthy tourists. Marisol grew up like everyone else—poor and silent and always cautious about who might be watching. ✸

CUBAN COMMUNISM

The concept of Communism is built on the principle of public ownership, operation, and distribution of wealth. To achieve this, Fidel Castro took control of plantations, businesses, factories, and utilities and placed them in the hands of government. Everyone was guaranteed a common and equal standard of living. Communism actually improved life for the five million Cubans who had been kept poor by the series of Cuban dictators that protected the upper classes' wealth and privilege. Beginning in 1959, the government built schools, hospitals, factories, and apart- ments (replacing grass huts). Cubans enjoyed better health than ever before, but they could not vote or speak out against the government or choose where they would live or work. Food and clothing were rationed, and there were no luxuries at all. Monthly salaries were low, and goods were costly. The older Cubans appreciated having food, shelter, health care, and clothing because they had gotten nothing under the rule of dictators, but the younger Cubans didn't remember those hardships. They only knew that they didn't have things that other societies have.

The fishing boat *Mary Evelyn*
is packed with Cuban
refugees during the Mariel
boatlift in April 1980. This
short reprieve in Cuban
emigration policy changed
the lives of thousands
of people living under Cuba's
repressive system.

3   How Cubans Came to North America

Before the 1960s, Cubans did not immigrate in great numbers to anywhere, as did other nationalities, such as the Italians, Irish, Germans, or Scandinavians. They had no need to because the Cuban economy had been growing ever since Spain settled it in 1511. Those few Cubans who did immigrate to North and South America were generally merchants or educated political refugees or skilled workers. From 1860 to the 1880s, Cuban cigar factories in the U.S. prompted Cuban workers to immigrate. There were also ferryboats and steamships that made immigration to the Gulf and Atlantic coasts easy. Popular locations were New Orleans, Mobile, Pensacola, Tampa, Key West, Miami, Baltimore, Philadelphia, New York, and Boston. Furthermore, Cubans were free to travel back and forth as often as they liked, for the ferry from Cuba to Key West had no regulations and each state at that time made its own immigration laws.

During the Great Depression (1930s), the U.S. eliminated immigration quota restrictions, and more Cubans traveled freely and frequently between their island and the U.S. It was during that time that Marisol's Great-Uncle Juan and Great-Aunt Nina immigrated to New York City in style, arriving by steamship at the great West Side docks and beginning their new life with plenty of cash and resources. Also during that time, Great-Aunt Benita and her husband traveled back and forth from Cuba and the U.S. for months at a time, finding new food suppliers as they vacationed in various spots in the United States. When their son Roberto grew up, he continued the tradition with his wife and son Gustavo, taking long vacations in the U.S. while he searched for new products to bring to Cuba.

In October 1960, however, when it became clear to Gustavo's father that his business was going to be taken from his family, activity in the house changed. Winter clothes were searched for and packed. Jewelry and money were concealed and passed on for secret shipping with hopes it would reach them in the future. Gustavo's mother awoke him one day, and he saw the hallway lined with dozens of suitcases. They all left that day for the ferry—the same ferry that was the joyous beginning of their long U.S. vacations—where each bag was inspected before they got on the boat. His father, Roberto, normally cheerful and full of life, was silent and withdrawn as the ferry pulled away, taking them away from Cuba forever.

Until 1962, people were allowed to leave Cuba freely. But then Castro realized he was losing the best and brightest from Cuba. Talented, intelligent people were leaving the country and seeking a better life elsewhere. To slow down this "brain drain," he required proper documentation, such as a visa, to leave, and made them difficult to obtain. When someone did apply for a visa, he or she was immediately "exposed" as a counter-revolutionary. Then, they would lose their job and be sent to the fields to work until their visa was approved, if ever. Castro canceled regular flights to the U.S., only allowing planes to Mexico and Spain. Cubans who were eventually granted visas often traveled to Spain or Mexico in order to make an application to enter the U.S. for political or economic reasons. That step could add months, even years, to the immigration process. It was also expensive, which meant that only the rich could afford to immigrate.

The middle class and poor who did not like Castro would not be stopped from leaving. They would risk everything—including their lives—to leave the island. They would find or make small boats or even lash inner tubes together to attempt to cross the ocean to freedom. Between 1962 and 1965, 35,000 Cubans came to the United States by any means possible.

WILLIAM'S STORY OF SURVIVAL

There was no sun in the day, and big waves washed over us. We had to hang on. And it was cold at night. Soon the raft fell apart, and we grabbed the tires and wood to hold on to something. One of the women brought a dog that had to swim, but soon sank. Then everyone else began to die. The doctor was swimming as best he could when he said, "William, I can't do any more I hope God—" and disappeared through the center of the tire used as a life preserver. The remaining group tried to keep a circle, but another man sank to his death. Mother burst into tears. There were only two left. I made a small raft and pulled Mother up on it. Sun burned us, and we became delirious. We were hidden by waves, blending in with the water. Toward her end, Mother encouraged me to fight for my life, "Save yourself. Tell the world we died trying to be free. I'm going to sleep now, don't wake me."

A group of Cubans celebrate their arrival in America. Between April and October 1980, more than 125,000 Cubans came to the United States—a movement that became known as the Mariel boatlift.

In September 1965, the immigration policy was eased due to the beginning of **détente** between the United States and the Soviet Union. Cubans with relatives in the U.S. were allowed to emigrate if they were picked up by boat. Many boats came, and some sank on their journey home. Between October and November of that year, nearly 5,000 Cubans entered the U.S. by boat.

Because of the deaths from boat travel, the U.S. and Cuba again revised their policy. In an effort called Family Reunification Flights, lists were put together of those people who would be allowed to emigrate out of Cuba by authorized air flights to the U.S. Anyone with a critical job in Cuba had to wait. Those that did apply lost their jobs and worked in the fields for months or years to gain approval. With only two freedom flights a day, 3,000 to 4,000 people left Cuba each month. By late 1969, 230,000 Cubans had arrived in the US. That was the end of the approved *exodus*, however. In May 1969, the Cuban doors once again closed, and no new exit visas were granted.

This action on Castro's part led to what became known as "desperation transportation." By the 1970s, Cuba was on a fast road downhill. No new industry had been developed in the past decade and there were no new parts, materials, and knowledge to keep technology going due to an *embargo* imposed by other

FREEDOM

One Cuban escapee in 1972 had to navigate a treacherous path to reach the American Naval Base at Cuba's Guantanamo Bay. "We had to pass through three fortified fences placed by the Cuban government. For the first fence we waited all afternoon—hiding, cold, observing the passing of the guards. No moon at night. At 11:00 we crossed the first fence. There were horizontal wires every five inches. We used heavy ropes to pry them apart and crawled through. We rolled our bodies across the road to avoid detection. Then there were two more fences to pry our way through. Then the minefield. Across the ground was a very thin wire, barely visible. It was attached to a detonator, that when broken, would explode. We felt our way carefully. The next series of fences had less surveillance. Then we saw American guards. Climbing over the top of the chain-linked fence, we cried out in joy, "Finally, we've reached freedom."

A Cuban family stands together at their home in Miami, Florida. The nature of Cuba's emigration laws make it sometimes difficult to keep families connected and united.

non-Communist countries. These dismal conditions prompted people to leave any way they could. There are many horrific stories of people's journeys to escape the controlling Castro government with only a hope of a new and better life to sustain them.

Between 1973 and 1979, 38,000 emigrants left Cuba, with 26,000 going through a third-party country such as Mexico, Spain, Jamaica, or Venezuela. Most were headed for the United States to join other relatives.

By the late 1970s, a large percentage of Cuba's population had known nothing but socialism. They had been given a place to live and work and food to eat, no matter how meager. They were also fed much ***propaganda*** about the evilness of the world outside of Cuba. In spite of those tactics, people still risked their lives for freedom. In 1980, after many deaths from boats trying to cross to freedom and after 10,000 people stormed the Peruvian Embassy in Havana, including Marisol and her mother, demanding exit visas, Castro once again opened immigration. Eleven thousand people applied to fly to Peru even though Peru only offered to take 1,000. Bolivia, Venezuela, Columbia, and Ecuador agreed to take some immigrants as well. The U.S. volunteered to take 3,500. Everyone wanted to go to Miami, however. Then Castro decided to use this immigration to his advantage. He canceled flights, but allowed boats to land on Cuban shores and take people away. However, they would

also have to take away people Castro no longer wanted on Cuban shores, such as prisoners, prostitutes, and criminally insane patients. This exodus became known as the Mariel boatlift. Between April and September of 1980, the *flotilla* of boats brought over 125,000 refugees to Florida. Among them was Marisol—without her mother, without her aunt, and without knowing what would come next.

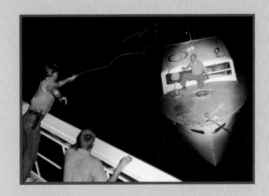

American coast guard sailors throw a line to a Cuban refugee stuck on his boat. Many Cubans have lost their lives in the hope of escaping the harsh government of Cuba.

An urban mural brightens up the street in Little Havana, Miami, Florida. Like many groups of immigrants, Cubans have found ways to preserve their culture within America.

4 Where They Settled

The first large group of Cuban immigrants in the 1860s settled where the Cuban cigar manufacturers had set up factories. These factories were built specifically to avoid a high *tariff* charged on their product when it was shipped to sell in the United States. Locating their cigar factories in U.S. cities, such as Key West and New York City, meant they wouldn't have to pay the tax. The factory owners also played a role in initiating a ferry service from Havana, Cuba, to Key West, Florida, which attracted more workers. In 1885, Vincente Martinez Ybor needed more room for his operation and opened up a plant near Tampa, which eventually became Ybor City, a town entirely devoted to cigar production and related products. By 1870, there were more than 45 factories in Key West making 25 million cigars a year—mostly by Cuban immigrants.

The next mass immigration was in the early 1960s. While today's Miami is a thriving metropolitan area, it was not so in the 1960s. When Disney World opened in Orlando—in the north of Florida—it caused 80 percent of the tourists who once drove further south (bringing their much-needed tourism dollars) to stop at the top of Florida. At the same time, airfares to Jamaica and Puerto Rico were reduced, making those destinations affordable to many more people in the U.S. In the 1960s, Miami was in the middle of an economic depression. Thus, when the Golden Exiles from Cuba immigrated to Miami, they found empty storefronts and boarded-up homes. The owners of these places welcomed these immigrants to fill the

Thousands of marchers show up in Little Havana, Miami, to protest the raid in which armed federal agents took Elian Gonzales from his home. The six-year-old had fled Cuba with his mother to stay with family in Florida.

economic vacuum in the area. Marisol's cousin, Gustavo, was one of many who settled in Miami to begin a new life in America.

Between 1959 and 1969, 400,000 Cubans immigrated to the United States. The U.S. government tried to resettle the exiles all over country. They were sent to Union City and West New York in New Jersey. They were sent to Denver and Minneapolis and Houston and St. Louis and Indiana, as well as New York and Pennsylvania and Boston. The 1970 Census documented Cubans in every state except Wyoming and Vermont.

The 2006 American Community Survey, a project of the U.S. Census Bureau, noted that 1,520,276 people identified themselves as Cuban-Americans. Most Cuban-Americans live in Florida, New York, New Jersey, California, or Illinois.

While exiled Cubans would initially agree to go wherever they were welcome—including the Midwest—the placements were often unsuccessful. Cubans are passionate about close-knit

family structures, often having parents, grandparents, and other relatives living close together. As a result, "chain migration" took over, causing the Cuban exiles to follow the routes of their predecessors and move to places where family and friends had settled. The "chain" for Cubans meant predominantly southern Florida, then New Jersey and New York. Miami's **proximity** to Cuba made it a logical place to land. Exiles stayed because its climate and region reminded them of their homeland. ✸

Little Havana in Miami, Florida, is a center of Cuban culture in the United States. These men in Little Havana's Domino Park are playing the game for which the park is named.

A colorfully costumed band marches through the streets of Little Havana, Miami, during the Calle Ocho Festival. Southern Florida is strongly influenced by Caribbean and Latin American culture.

5 Types of Work and How They Lived

Unlike other immigrant groups, who were often looked upon with *circumspect* and caution when they arrived in the United States, the Cubans had always been viewed as skilled, educated, politically conservative, hard working, and law abiding.

From the 1860s to the 1920s, cigar factories led to the workers developing their own related businesses, such as cigar box and label manufacturing, running boarding homes for workers, laundries, and grocery stores. As the Florida tourist areas grew, Cubans worked in the construction of hotels and homes and related service jobs. Agriculture also provided immigrants with jobs, harvesting sugarcane, avocados, and tropical fruit.

In the 1930s, Ybor City was a focused Cuban-American area, having been developed and built by a cigar manufacturer. He built in services for his workers, including social clubs, libraries, art classes, auditoriums, gyms, dance halls, and canteens. This city became a regular venue for singers and theater performers, including international performers, such as the famous opera tenor Enrico Caruso.

During the 1940s and 1950s, poor Cubans left their homeland because jobs were scarce. They may not have known much English, but they were hard workers and often got jobs in restaurants and hotels. Cuban life in New York was centered regular gatherings at

CUBAN BUSINESSES IN AMERICA
In the 1960s, 10 percent of all Miami businesses were Cuban-owned. Not only were they establishing an income for their family, they were also providing a place for new immigrants to work. Unlike many other Hispanic cultures, the Cuban women worked outside the home and traditionally gave birth to fewer babies, creating less financial strain on the family. Cuban families stressed education for their children and enjoyed a social mobility unknown to other immigrant groups at the time. By 1970, Cuban-owned businesses had the highest gross annual receipts compared with any other recent immigrant groups.

restaurants, barbershops, and cafes. La Salle, a cafeteria on the corner of Seventh and Fifty-first streets, was a popular meeting spot for musicians and show-business people from Cuba.

When the Golden Exiles landed in the United States in the 1960s, they were the best-educated and wealthiest group. Many were professionals, such as doctors, lawyers, bankers, business owners, and professors. They faced a language and cultural barrier, however, and were often forced to take jobs as garment workers, janitors, maids, and factory workers. While in Cuba, these privileged people would have had the luxury of the wife staying at home, often to supervise the house staff, while the husband was the sole money earner. However, after immigrating, everyone in the family worked.

This group of Cubans was treated well by the U.S. government, which arranged for monthly allowances for the needy. There were also

Cuban-born entertainer Desi Arnaz hugs his wife, the comedian Lucille Ball. The two starred in the popular television show *I Love Lucy*. Arnaz was one of the first Cuban-American performers to be so successful.

many programs to help them integrate into the community, learn English, transfer their professional knowledge and credentials into U.S. standards, as well as go to school. Between 1961 and 1971, the federal government contributed 730 million dollars to Cuban aid. Thirty-four million went to 16,000 college students, and 130 million went to bilingual and multicultural awareness programs.

While this group of immigrants had unique problems due to their upper-class background, they were also highly motivated to meet the challenges of language and cultural barriers. They initially thought that Castro would be quickly defeated and they would reclaim their former lives, however, it soon became clear that was not meant to be. Thus, Cuban Americans began rebuilding their lives on U.S. soil.

Carlos Gutierrez came to America with his family in 1960, when he was six years old. After a successful business career, in 2005, Gutierrez was appointed to a high government position, U.S. Secretary of Commerce.

Singer Gloria Estefan has had a long career
marked by adversity and triumph.

Between 1960 and 1970, Eighth Street in Miami became lined with
Cuban-owned restaurants, supermarkets, gas stations, bakeries,
florists, fruit stands, barbershops, car dealerships, furniture show-
rooms, appliance stores, funeral parlors, and schools. While it was
called "Little Havana," it was actually better than the real Havana
because of its abundance of food and freedom. ✳

6 Exile vs. Immigrant vs. Citizen

Marisol's cousin Gustavo was only a young boy when he was exiled to America. In Cuba, Gustavo's father was an important man who was well known and respected. However, in America, he was a nobody and had to struggle to put food on the table. Gustavo's father clung to the hope of someday returning to the Cuba he once knew. He never developed American expectations for his family because he never chose to come to America. He was exiled to America, thrown out of the life he wanted into one he did not. An *exile* is always looking back with longing.

In contrast, most *immigrants* come to a new country to start all over. They leave their country by choice in the hopes of having a better life somewhere else. Immigrants are usually looking forward to building a better life than the one they left behind.

Unique to the Cuban exile experience is their closeness to their former home but their inability to go back, not even for a visit. While many Cubans still hold onto the notion that Castro will be overthrown and they will return, many others have gradually let go

Cuban refugees arrive in Florida. Exiles and immigrants from Cuba can become citizens of the United States in the hopes of creating a better life in a new country.

of that dream and moved psychologically from being an exile to an immigrant, and then ultimately becoming a *citizen* of the U.S.

The 2006 American Community Survey, a project of the U.S. Census Bureau, reported that more than 1.5 million people identify themselves as Cuban American. Florida—in particular, the Miami area—is home to more than a million Cuban Americans, two-thirds of the nation's total.

A Cuban man holds the American flag at a citizenship ceremony. Three thousand people attended this ceremony and took the Oath of Allegiance, swearing their loyalty to the United States.

The number of Cuban Americans in Canada is much smaller, estimated at about 18,000 people in 2008. Cuban communities have thrived in such cities as Toronto and Montreal.

Today, there is new hope that the relationship between Cuba and the United States will be opened again after decades of communist rule. Many Cuban Americans look forward to a time when travel restrictions and economic sanctions will be lifted. Marisol and many other Cuban Americans hope one day to visit Cuba and find that it once again is a land of plenty. ✹

SECTION

3

Famous Cuban Immigrants

Orlando Hernandez: El Duque

Born in Communist Cuba in October 1969, Orlando Hernandez was the son of a baseball player called "El Duque." At an early age he demonstrated a talent for pitching, as did his stepbrother Livan. While professional sports are outlawed in Cuba, the national baseball team is a source of pride. With his unique pitching style, Orlando was accepted on the national team. The baseball job entitled him to a small salary, house, car, and meals. He married and had a daughter. In 1992, his pitching helped Cuba win the first Olympic baseball event. In 1994, his stepbrother Livan joined the national team but did not receive the same benefits as Orlando. Livan was discontent and asked Orlando to **defect** with him. Orlando declined, however, because he was expecting another child. In 1995, while in Mexico practicing for international games, Livan defected to the United States. Back in Cuba, Livan's action put Orlando under severe scrutiny. He was questioned and eventually dropped from the team so that he would not have the opportunity to defect when the team went to Atlanta for the Olympics in 1996. He was treated like a criminal while his stepbrother Livan lived in great success in the United States with a four-million-dollar baseball contract. On December 25, 1997, he and five friends decided to escape Cuba by boat. Soon after reaching the United States, Orlando signed a contract with the New York Yankees. Since then he has been one of baseball's best pitchers.

Gloria Estefan: Queen of Latin Pop

Life in the United States was difficult for Gloria when she arrived from Cuba. She was shy and overweight, with few friends. But she studied hard, mastered English quickly, and was on the school honor roll each year. The next big difficulty for Gloria was when her father became seriously ill. Confined to bed, he was dependent on 10-year-old Gloria to help him, as her mother had to work to earn money for the family. Gloria spent much of her free time at home with her father. She listened and sang to music and learned to play the acoustic guitar. At 16, she organized a band, and when she heard a man speak about music at her high school, she was inspired to meet him. That was the first time she met Emilio Estefan, who would later become her husband. In 1980, Gloria's father died, and Emilio decided to quit his job and get a record deal for the band—The Miami Sound Machine. He did, and the band went on to great success throughout the '80s and '90s as they brought the Latin sound to the popular markets.

Emilio Estefan Jr.: Founder/Producer of Miami Sound Machine

Born in 1952, Emilio's family left Cuba in 1965, fleeing to Spain before entering the U.S. in 1967. Emilio was 15. He was a hard worker from the beginning: delivering groceries, selling T-shirts, making sashes, being a mail clerk for Barcardi Imports. His love of music began at age six when he got an accordion for Christmas. Before the family even left Cuba, he was entertaining local diners with popular songs played on the accordion. In the United States he found two other musicians—a drummer and a conga player—and began working parties and dance clubs. Their reputation spread quickly. Emilio first met Gloria when she asked for pointers for her high school girl band. He was immediately attracted to her, but said nothing. They met again at a wedding Gloria attended at which his band was playing. She sang at the wedding and was a big hit, leading to her joining the band in 1975. From that point on, their fate together was sealed. In 1980, Emilio decided to stop performing and produce the band's activities. Under his vision and direction, the band has become an international success.

Andy Garcia: Actor

In 1961, when Andy was five years old, he heard gunfire in Havana from the failed U.S. invasion of Cuba at the Bay of Pigs. He was told the family would leave for Miami as soon as possible. Once in Miami, his father began a food catering business, while his mother worked as a secretary. His father sold the business and took up the new business of selling hosiery. As Andy grew up, he participated in the family business. After school and baseball practice, he would take a 45-minute bus ride to his father's warehouse to sweep the floors and then ride home with his father. Andy attended Florida International University. When he auditioned for his first play, he recognized his true calling in life. In 1978, he left Miami for Hollywood to seek success in the world of acting. It was a long, hard climb, and many agents wanted him to change his appearance to be less Hispanic looking. Andy would not do that, however, and finally got his big break in 1985. He is now a recognized and well-respected actor.

Desi Arnez: Musician, Singer, Producer, Husband of Lucille Ball

Born on March 2, 1917, Desi was the only son of a prominent Cuban family. They came to the United States in 1934 and moved to Miami, where Desi finished high school, played football, and befriended the son of mob gangster, Al Capone. He worked odd jobs, such as cleaning birdcages, and also sang at a Miami Beach nightclub. While singing, he was spotted by bandleader Xavier Cugat, who asked Desi to sing for him. Soon, Desi formed his own band and introduced the conga drums to the American music scene through the nightclub circuit. While in New York, he met the Broadway director George Abbott, who cast him in "Too Many Girls," a Rogers and Hart musical. At age 23, he was cast to play the same role in a motion picture version of the play. During World War II, he served in the U.S. Army by performing in the touring USO shows that entertained the troops overseas. In 1946, he returned to the movie and music business. While he acted in a half-dozen movies, he was never a great singer or dancer. He was, however, a good showman and businessman. Desi used his sharp business *acumen* to transform Desilu Productions into a successful television production company. His character on the T.V. show *I Love Lucy* was the single most visible Hispanic presence in U.S. television for many years. A majority of Americans got their ideas about Cubans' behavior, speech, and temper by watching *I Love Lucy*.

Perez Prado: King of the Mambo

The mambo was not particularly popular in Cuba, but it became very popular in America because of a Cuban musician. While there were many salsa-style musicians who came from Cuba, Perez Prado is considered the person responsible for creating the mambo sound and dance. Unlike the rumba, mambo did not come from a long-standing tradition of dancing spontaneously in the street. Mambos were created in dance halls. Perez was born in the Cuban province of Matanzas in 1916 and moved to Havana in 1942. Playing small clubs initially, he joined an orchestra playing the piano and making the music arrangements until 1949. He then left Cuba for Mexico and recorded his experimental blend of big band and Afro-Cuban rhythms—from which the mambo was born. Success visited him quickly, making him $5,000 a week from playing and recording mambo music. Tito Puente and other mambo players also gained fame because of Prado's music.

Immigration Figures

**Cuban Americans living in the United States
(no figures available before 1860)**

1860:   5,772

1860:   7,353

1870:   5,319

1880:   6,917

1890   23,256 (mixed with other West Indies population)

1900:   11,081

1910:   15,133

1920:   14,872

1930:   18,493

1940:   (no figures available)

1950:   (no figures available)

1960:   79,150

1970:   439,048

1980:   803,226

1990:   1,056,080

2000:   1,228,149

2008:   1,520,276

Sources: U.S. Census Bureau; 2006 American Community Survey

Glossary

Acumen quickness of mental perception; keen insight.

Century one hundred years; the grouping of years beginning with 00 and ending with 99.

Circumspect wary, watchful, cautious.

Communism a philosophy of economics that prohibits private ownership and demands that everyone share equally in the work and the wealth.

Cost of living the money needed to maintain a certain lifestyle, usually based on basic needs such as food, shelter and clothing.

Defect a choice to leave a country that does not allow its citizens the freedom to leave.

Détente a move toward peace between two competing entities (such as people or countries) with a mutual reduction of aggressive behavior.

Discontent unhappy, unsatisfied.

Economic relations the money-based transactions between two parties.

Elite the socially superior part of a society.

Embargo a government act forbidding vessels to enter or leave ports, or a stoppage of trade.

Exodus a mass departure.

Flotilla a fleet of ships or boats.

Gross annual receipts the total amount of income before the deduction of expenses.

Immigrate to come to a country as a permanent resident.

Majority the preponderant quality or share.

Mass exile a large group of people forced to leave their native country.

Oblivious forgetful, absorbed, distracted.

Peddler a person who sells items from door to door or on the street.

Police state a controlled environment where the police are the most powerful entities.

Propaganda the spreading of ideas, information, or rumors for the purpose of helping or injuring an institution, a cause, or a person.

Proximity immediate nearness in place, time, or other relation.

Tariff a tax levied by the government on imports and/or exports.

Turmoil disturbance, agitation.

Visa a stamp on a passport indicating that a person has approval to enter a country.

Further Reading

About the Cuban Americans

Cieslik, Thomas, et al, editors. *Immigration: A Documentary and Reference Guide.* Westport, Conn.: Greenhaven Press, 2008.

Herrera, Andrea O'Reilly, editor. *Remembering Cuba: Legacy of a Diaspora.* Austin: University of Texas Press, 2001.

Hoobler, Dorothy and Thomas Hoobler. *The Cuban American Family Album.* New York: Oxford University Press, 1996.

Jatar-Hausmann, Ana Julia. *The Cuban Way: Capitalism, Communism, and Confrontation.* Bloomfield, Conn.: Kumarian Press, 1999.

Marcovitz, Hal. *The Cuban Americans.* Philadelphia: Mason Crest, 2008.

O'Donnell, Liam. *U.S. Immigration.* Mankato, Minn.: Capstone Press, 2008.

Perez Firmat, Gustavo. *Next Year in Cuba.* New York: Anchor Books, Bantam, Doubleday, Dell Publishing Group, 1995.

Torres, Maria de los Angeles. *In the Land of Mirrors: Cuban Exile Policy in the United States.* Ann Arbor: University of Michigan Press, 2000.

Finding your Cuban American ancestors

Carmack, Sharon DeBartolo. *A Geneaologist's Guide to Discovering Your Immigrant and Ethnic Ancestors.* Cincinnati: Betterway Books, 2000.

Platt, Lyman D. *Census Records for Latin America and the Hispanic United States.* Baltimore: Genealogical Publishing Co., 1998.

Ryskamp, George. *Finding Your Hispanic Roots.* Baltimore: Genealogical Publishing Co., 1997.

Internet Resources

http://www.census.gov

The official Web site of the U.S. Census Bureau contains information about the most recent census, taken in 2000.

http://www12.statcan.ca/english/census/index.cfm

The Web site for Canada's Bureau of Statistics, which includes population information updated for the most recent census in May 2006.

http://www.usimmigrationsupport.org/cubaimmigration.html

A brief synopsis of Cuban immigration to the United States.

http://www.cuban-exile.com/index.shtml

This extensive Web site is dedicated to exploring the historical relationship between Cuba and the United States. It also provides links to contemporary news articles.

http://www.cubanfest.com/mission.htm

The official Web site of the Cuban American Heritage Festival, which seeks to preserve the rich history and heritage of Cuban immigrants to America.

Index

Photo Credits

Page

2: Papilio/Corbis
10: Arne Hodalic/Corbis
13: Hulton/Archive
14: Tom Bean/Corbis
17: Papilio/Corbis
18: Hulton/Archive
21: Hulton/Archive
22: Hulton/Archive
27: Hulton/Archive
30: Hulton/Archive
34: Hulton/Archive

36: Hulton/Archive
37: Hulton/Archive
38: Robert Holmes/Corbis
41: Hulton/Archive
42: Nik Wheeler/Corbis
44: Nik Wheeler/Corbis
47: Hulton/Archive
48: U.S. Department of Commerce
49: Hulton/Archive
50: Hulton/Archive
53: Hulton/Archive

Contributors

Barry Moreno has been librarian and historian at the Ellis Island Immigration Museum and the Statue of Liberty National Monument since 1988. He is the author of *The Statue of Liberty Encyclopedia*, which was published by Simon and Schuster in October 2000. He is a native of Los Angeles, California. After graduation from California State University at Los Angeles, where he earned a degree in history, he joined the National Park Service as a seasonal park ranger at the Statue of Liberty; he eventually became the monument's librarian. In his spare time, Barry enjoys reading, writing, and studying foreign languages and grammar. His biography has been included in *Who's Who Among Hispanic Americans, The Directory of National Park Service Historians, Who's Who in America,* and *The Directory of American Scholars.*

Laura Hahn is a creative writing teacher for young people and a freelance writer of articles, stories, plays, and business copy. Earlier in her career, she worked as a professional writer and communicator for corporations. Her favorite writing work focuses on understanding how human beings achieve their dreams, especially when it comes to making a difference and following their bliss.